D0938586

U.S. ★ WARPLANES

THE B-52 STRATOFORTRESS

Meg Greene

the rosen publishing group's
rosen central

For Jordy, Isaac, and Toby

Published in 2003 by The Rosen Publishing Group, Inc.
29 East 21st Street, New York, NY 10010

First Edition

Library of Congress Cataloging-in-Publication Data

Greene, Meg.
The B-52 Stratofortress / by Meg Greene.
    p. cm. — (U.S. warplanes)
Summary: Discusses history of the B-52 Stratofortress warplane and its use in the military campaigns in Afghanistan after the September 11, 2001, terrorist attacks. Includes bibliographical references and index.
ISBN 0-8239-3872-7 (library binding)
1. B-52 bomber—History—Juvenile literature. [1. B-52 bomber—History.
2. Bombers—History.] I. Title. II. Series.
UG1242.B6 G713 2003
623.7'463—dc21

                                                                2002007952

Manufactured in the United States of America

CONTENTS

A B-52 on the ramp at RAF Fairford, United Kingdom, being prepared for a strike over former Yugoslavia in May 1999. These huge aircraft had both the bomb bay and external weapons pylons loaded with cluster bombs, 500-pound (227-kilogram) "iron" bombs, and AGM-142s (air-to-ground missiles).

In an industry not known for its long-lasting designs, the staying power of the B-52 Stratofortress is legendary. Since its first appearance in 1952, the B-52 has been the backbone of American air defense. Affectionately known as BUFFs, or Big Ugly Fat Fellows, by those who fly them, the B-52 has been in constant use for half a century.

The current model and eighth in the B-52 series, the B-52H—first introduced in 1962—is now more than forty years old. The plane is capable of strategically dropping the widest range of weapons available, including free-fall bombs, cluster bombs, and precision guided missiles. This ability makes the B-52 among the most versatile and dependable airplanes ever created.

Despite its age, the plane continues to distinguish itself. Designed for use during the Cold War, the B-52H remained in service throughout the Vietnam War (1962–1975), Operation Desert Storm (1990–1991), and the Kosovo War (1999), and it is now part of Operation Enduring Freedom in Afghanistan. In fact, the B-52H saw more combat in the 1990s than in the previous three decades combined. As one expert has suggested, the B-52 is "the plane that never stops." Currently, the plane is scheduled to be retired in 2040. If so, the B-52 will have been in service for 90 years, making it one of the longest serving frontline combat aircraft in the world.

An American Symbol

The world for which the B-52H was made has changed dramatically since it entered service in 1962. The tensions of the Cold War, in which the United States and the Soviet Union eyed each other with suspicion and fear, disappeared when the Soviet Union collapsed in

The SR-71 Blackbird was developed to aid U.S. reconnaissance during the Cold War and carried no weapons. Clocking in at a speed of over three times the speed of sound, the SR-71 was the fastest and highest-flying plane ever designed for the U.S. Air Force. It once flew from New York to London in less than two hours. Although it was retired by President Clinton in 1997, the air force still owns six Blackbirds for research purposes.

1991. Although as of 2002 there are only ninety-two B-52s still in use, out of the 744 built by the Boeing Company, the B-52H is still the key to American air defense, ready to go at a moment's notice. Other planes, such as the F-100 Supersabre and the B-29 Superfortress, which were also used during the Cold War period, have since been retired and are seen only at air and space museums or air shows. At a time when technology changes at lightning speed, and the notion of keeping anything for a long period of time seems old-fashioned, the B-52 endures.

Solid, reliable, and sturdy, the B-52H is the workhorse of the U.S. Air Force. Not as sleek or high-tech as the B-2 Spirits or the F/A-18 Hornets, the BUFFs continue to inspire pride in the engineers who designed them, the pilots and crews who operate them, and the technicians and mechanics who keep them flying.

For countless Americans, the B-52 has become a symbol of freedom, always ready to defend the United States and protect its interests. For others around the world, the B-52 has a more uncertain meaning. People who are friendly with the United States admire and respect the power the B-52s represent. But America's enemies hate and fear it, for the B-52 is an awe-inspiring weapon that continues to represent American might.

On Sunday, October 7, 2001, less than a month after the terror attacks of September 11 on the United States, the leaders at the Pentagon ordered the B-52H Stratofortress into battle. Throughout the night, British and American ships launched repeated air strikes against Afghanistan in retaliation for harboring terrorists, especially Osama bin Laden. Bin Laden is the man U.S. officials believe is responsible for the September 11, 2001, attacks on New York City and Washington, D.C., as well as previous bombings of the World Trade Center in 1993 and the U.S. Embassies in Kenya and Tanzania, Africa, in 1998.

Smoke rises from the snowy mountains of Tora Bora in eastern Afghanistan following a B-52 attack on Al Qaeda and Taliban strongholds.

Going to War

The first wave of assaults began about 8:45 PM local time, as B-52H Stratofortresses, joined by B-1 and B-2 Stealth bombers, blasted the Afghan cities of Kandahar, Kabul, Jalalabad, and Herat. Targets included airfields, military bases, radar systems, the Taliban (an extreme Islamic group that formerly ruled Afghanistan and supported

"A BARGAIN BOMBER"

One of the reasons the B-52 Stratofortress has become such an important part of American military strategy in Afghanistan is that, compared to other planes, it is the most cost-effective heavy bomber in American military history. Aside from being the least expensive plane to maintain, it also has the lowest accident rate, making it the safest ship in the air fleet.

Besides its ability to carry different types of weaponry, the B-52H can stay in the air for long periods of time. Based on the island of Diego Garcia in the Indian Ocean, which is located just south of India, the B-52s can easily make the approximately sixteen-hour round trip to Afghanistan. Because it can refuel in the air, the B-52 can fly anywhere in the world with a payload of bombs or missiles. Once over Afghanistan, the planes, carrying up to a dozen 2,000-pound (approximately 910 kilograms) bombs, can circle a combat zone for hours, waiting for the ground forces or air force controllers to send them the exact coordinates of a target. More than 90 percent of the time, bombs dropped from a B-52H landed within 50 feet (15.3 meters) of the targeted location.

the terrorist group Al Qaeda and Osama bin Laden), the defense ministry, airport-based command centers, and electrical power lines and power plants. The raids continued well into the following day.

In a speech to the American people, as quoted in an article in *Jane's Defence Weekly*, President George W. Bush stated: "The United States military has begun strikes against Al Qaeda terrorist training camps and military installations of the Taliban regime." The operations, Bush said, "are designed to disrupt the use of Afghanistan as a terrorist base of operations and to attack the military capabilities of the Taliban." To achieve this goal, U.S. military officials once again turned to the B-52 as an essential component of their strategy.

To date, the B-52 Stratofortress has proved to be one of the most effective weapons in the American arsenal. Since the beginning of Operation Enduring Freedom, B-52 bombers, along with B-2 Spirits and B-1 Lancers, have dropped approximately 80 percent of the bombs used in the war against Taliban and Al Qaeda forces in Afghanistan. In addition, B-52s have also provided air support for U.S. ground forces.

Operation Desert Storm was one of the first U.S. military conflicts to take place on an area as open as the Iraqi desert. The B-52H shown here is from Barksdale AFB, Louisiana. That is where President Bush first went in Air Force One on September 11, 2001, after the attacks in New York and on the Pentagon, before flying on to Offut AFB, Nebraska, and then to Washington.

Carpet Bombing

Although the B-52 Stratofortress has been successful in launching precision bombs, that has not been its main role in Operation Enduring Freedom. Since November 2001, the planes have been used in carpet-bombing operations. Carpet bombing requires that a single bomber drop large numbers of 500-pound (or approximately 225 kilograms) "dumb" or cluster bombs on the same target area, which in many cases can be the size of a football field. Military analysts believe that carpet bombing is effective because bombs are dropped with greater precision on one general target area instead of more haphazardly in a number of areas.

Yet despite improvements in accuracy, there is still the problem of bombs that land but do not explode. Unexploded bombs are a

---

CLUSTER BOMBS

Cluster bombs are some of the more dangerous weapons used by B-52s. When they explode, cluster bombs release a number of smaller bombs, often called bomblets. The range of the bomblets is such that a number of different targets in an area are hit. While cluster bombs can cover a large area, they are not always very accurate. They sometimes do not explode upon impact, and, like land mines, they are capable of exploding hours, days, and even years later, wounding or killing whoever happens to be close to the explosion, including civilians and friendly troops.

---

great threat to civilians. In addition, critics of carpet bombing have also pointed out that even with heavy bomb tonnage dropped on Taliban infantry targets, the enemy is so well hidden in caves that the bombing has been of limited success. There was at least one incident in which the tracking systems used on a B-52H were faulty, resulting in bombs being dropped on American soldiers instead of Taliban and Al Qaeda forces.

But the use of B-52s for carpet bombing has its supporters, too, such as the leaders of the Northern Alliance, who believe that the earlier bombing missions were not helping them in their fight against the Taliban and Al Qaeda. Carpet-bombing raids helped to open the way for Northern Alliance and American ground forces to take Kabul, the capital city of Afghanistan and once a Taliban and Al Qaeda stronghold.

Spreading the Message

The B-52 Stratofortress also carries the "mail bomb." Mail bombs consist of a metal casing that holds thousands of leaflets filled with propaganda messages designed to scare the enemy and spread messages of support to civilians and friendly forces. The war in Afghanistan is the first time that the B-52H has been used to drop mail bombs.

In the war against the Taliban, the B-52 warplanes not only dropped bombs over Afghan villages but also packages of food and propaganda leaflets. The leaflet held by this Afghan citizen offers a reward of $25 million for Osama bin Laden *(far right)*. The food drops were sometimes problematic because the locals mistook the packages for unexploded cluster bombs, which were the same yellow color.

The B-52 Stratofortress quickly earned a reputation among the Afghan people, especially those fighting the Taliban and Al Qaeda. Trying to bring peace to their country, Afghans warn each other about "B-52 justice," which means that those Afghans who oppose the United States or its allies stand a good chance of seeing their villages or towns destroyed by the planes.

Enemy troops have admitted that once they learned of the abilities of the B-52, they became discouraged and no longer wished to fight the Americans. When enemy soldiers noticed American soldiers looking at them with binoculars, they soon discovered that they had approximately ten minutes to run away or die. They were being targeted for a B-52 strike. Even those who sought refuge in caves soon realized how important it was to have more than one exit once they saw that bombs from the B-52s could permanently close the main one.

At the time of the publication of this book, the B-52 Stratofortress continues to fly missions over Afghanistan. Although the plane has played an important role in disrupting the Taliban government and scattering Al Qaeda forces, much remains to be done. As one squadron commander put it in an article written for the Air Combat Command News Service: "[The war] is not over. We are only on mile one of this . . . marathon against terrorism. But they [the enemy] are out there, and they already know about your capability and what you've done. You've taken it home to the Taliban and Al Qaeda, and believe me, you have made a difference."

The B-52H Stratofortresses used in Afghanistan are older than many of the pilots who fly them. Even though the B-52H is no longer being manufactured, it should continue to see plenty of action for years to come, thanks in part to careful maintenance (which ensures that the plane and its parts are safe) and continual upgrading to outfit the plane with the newest technology available.

Back to the Future

Boarding a B-52H is a little like going into and out of a time machine. The basic components of the plane—the ribs, fuselage, and wings—are all original. What has changed is the different systems that allow the plane to carry out the various functions assigned to it.

In the cockpit, the old instrument panel still has the original electromechanical gauges from the 1960s. These monitor the eight jet engines. By watching a small white needle as it moves back and forth, the pilot can see how the engines are working. There are small black plastic knobs and small warning lights that blink when engines are in trouble—all of which date from the plane's earliest days.

A closer inspection of the cockpit, however, reveals some significant changes. Many of the planes have "eyes" that were installed in the 1970s. The left "eye" is a low-light television camera that monitors images, while the right "eye" is a sophisticated imaging system that tracks and pinpoints targets. The wings and the fuselage have been reinforced to enable the planes to operate at low altitudes in an effort to escape radar. As one Boeing project manager happily stated in *Fast Company* magazine: "We like to say, 'The only thing old about the B-52 is the name.'"

The interior of a B-52 Stratofortress, where an air force flight crew is positioned at the controls. A red light illuminates the instrument panel.

A Closer Look at the BUFF

The original design of the B-52 guaranteed long-term adaptability. The B-52H Stratofortress in use today is still a long-range, high-altitude, heavy bomber that can perform a variety of missions just as it was originally designed to do fifty years ago. It is the only plane that can fire air-launched cruise missiles, also known as ALCMs, as well as carry a payload of up to 60,000 pounds (approximately 27,000 kilograms). Until 1991, the plane was equipped with a remote-control tail turret armed with either four .50-caliber machine guns or a 20-millimeter multibarrel cannon to protect it from an air attack. With the aid of advanced electronic systems and radar, the B-52H can even fly low-level, long-range missions under bad weather conditions.

The B-52H has a wingspan of 185 feet (56.4 meters), with each wing measuring approximately 2,000 square feet, or roughly the size of a three-bedroom house. The plane is 159 feet 4 inches (48.5 meters) long and 40 feet 8 inches (12.4 meters) high. Maximum take-off weight is 488,000 pounds (approximately 219,600 kilograms). It is powered by eight Pratt & Whitney TF33-P-3 turbofan engines, each delivering up to 17,000 pounds of thrust (the force produced by the engines). The B-52H can attain a top speed of nearly 600 miles per hour (965.6 kilometers per hour) and has a maximum range of 8,800 miles (14,080 kilometers) unfueled and a service ceiling of 50,000 feet (15,240 meters).

During wartime, the B-52H can carry out strategic attacks, prevention maneuvers, and offensive air and sea operations. The plane is highly effective when used for ocean surveillance and has the capability to assist the U.S. Navy in antiship and mine-laying operations. In just two hours, two B-52s can monitor 140,000 square miles (364,000 square kilometers) of ocean surface.

All B-52s are equipped with an electro-optical viewing system that uses infrared and high-resolution low-light television sensors to help with targeting, battle assessment, and flight safety, thus further improving its combat and low-level flight abil-

The B-52's eight engines allow it to fly at high subsonic speeds, a remarkable achievement for a plane carrying a heavy payload.

ities. Pilots wear night vision goggles (NVGs) during night operations. The goggles provide greater safety during night operations by increasing the pilot's ability to survey the terrain, avoid enemy radar, and see other aircraft under secret, lights-out missions.

Making Old BUFFs New

In order to keep the B-52 airworthy and its engines in top working order, a constant schedule of maintenance is required.

Another key to the success of the B-52H is that the planes currently in use are still relatively new in terms of flying time. The B-52H Stratofortresses used in Afghanistan were built in the early 1960s. But instead of seeing action in Vietnam, as did the earlier models of the B-52 such as the F and G series, the H series stood at "nuclear alert," ready to deploy in the event of a nuclear attack against the United States. Compared to other military planes, the B-52H, even with its heavy use in Afghanistan, logs an average of only 395 flight hours per aircraft. That amount of time is equal to what an ordinary passenger jet may fly in a month, and this has helped to cut down on the wear and tear the plane suffers.

Beginning in 1989, the air force, working with the Boeing Company, began a series of modifications to the B-52H to keep it current with other planes. The latest B-52H modification program began in 1994 and was designed to adapt the B-52H for more conventional, or standard, wartime duties as a bomber. While the air force had originally planned for the B-52G—an earlier model in the series—to be outfitted with the new modifications, the decision was eventually made to retire the G series due to funding cutbacks and the START (Strategic Arms Reduction Talks) agreements between the United States and Russia,

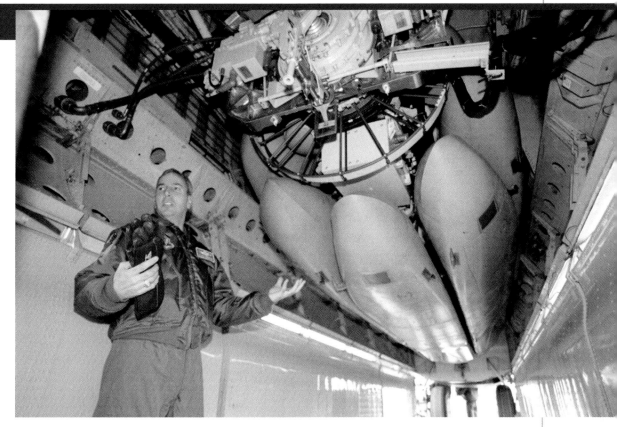

Built with the sole purpose of sinking enemy ships in mind, Harpoon missiles are commonly carried by the B-52 and were used frequently during Operation Desert Storm. Once enough information is acquired about a target, the Harpoon locks onto it. After it is fired, the Harpoon finds its destination with no further help from the crew.

which limited the number of strategic bombers (among other things) to be used. The B-52H, which was then restricted to use in a nuclear emergency, was pressed into service to take over some of the more conventional warfare duties that its older counterparts had carried out.

The first stage in the process was the addition of AGM-142 and Harpoon missiles to the B-52H, made possible by adding a Heavy Stores Adapter Beam (HSAB)—a specially constructed support beam—to the underwing weapons pylon. This innovation allowed the B-52H to carry weapons that were too long or too heavy to be accommodated on the standard I-beam rack adapter. In addition, the Heavy Stores Adapter Beam made it possible to carry up to nine large weapons on each pylon externally, depending on what kind of missile or weapon the plane was carrying. Also, a state-of-the-art global positioning system (GPS) was installed. These specially designed radar systems help pinpoint targets

"JUST LIKE HOME"

Plane designers put a lot of thought into crew comfort when building the B-52H. In the older planes, heat was unevenly distributed, and the pilots were frequently too warm while the navigators located on the bottom deck froze. The new design featured better heating for the lower deck. The uncomfortable seats, too, were updated to help reduce fatigue during a long mission. Finally, new hot cups for making soup or coffee, as well as new water outlets and relief (toilet) tubes, were added.

with greater accuracy. The use of aerial refueling gives the B-52 a range limited only by the endurance of the crew.

Manning the BUFF

The crew of the B-52H originally consisted of six members situated between the plane's two decks. The pilot and copilot sat side by side on the upper flight deck, with the pilot on the left. Behind them on the upper flight deck were the electronic warfare officer and the gunner, seated side by side and facing the rear. All four of these crew members sat in upward-firing ejector seats. The radar navigator, who was responsible for weapons delivery and for guiding the aircraft past dangerous terrain while flying at low altitude, and the navigator, who was responsible for getting the aircraft to its destination, sat facing forward side by side in the lower fuselage deck. This deck, known as "the hellhole," was a windowless chamber located in the bottom of the plane. Both of these crewmen sat on downward-firing ejector seats.

In October 1991, the gunner's station was removed as an economy measure, since the position of gunner was no longer needed. This reduced the number of crew members to only five. The gunner's ejector seat was, however, retained and can now be occupied by an instructor or flight examiner who often goes along on training missions. The M61A1 Vulcan 20 mm cannon in the tail section was taken out between 1991 and 1994, and the gun opening was covered over by a perforated (punched with holes) metal plate. Still, the wiring and instruments for the gun have been retained so that the gun can be reinstalled if necessary.

How to Keep BUFFs Flying

During the 1980s, the B-52Hs underwent major upgrades. All of the original bomb and navigation equipment was removed and replaced with more modern technology, including onboard computers, updated transmitting equipment, and encoding devices. One maintenance chief who worked to install the new equipment recalled in *Fast Company* magazine that with the older gear removed, the

As missile and bomb technology advances, aerial combat between planes becomes less common. As a result, the gunner's position on the B-52 has been removed, and the space the gun used to occupy is covered with a plate.

space "was as big as a dance hall." He added, "There were so many wires, I thought we'd never get it back together."

Although new engines have not been added to the B-52s, every four years each plane is stripped down to the bare metal and inspected for corrosion, rust, or worn-out parts. Nothing is spared as engines, tails, landing gear, bomb-bay doors, wing flaps, and the metal panels of "skin" are painstakingly removed. Such extensive maintenance is planned two years in advance, with as many as six to nine planes worked on at a time. According to records, a single plane requires 30,000 hours of work, with a timetable for completion of repairs that must not exceed 180 days in order that the next plane

The molds and jigs for many of the parts for the B-52 were destroyed in 1962, but the USAF has been able to draw on a sizable reserve of spare parts from aircraft stored at AMARC (The Aerospace Maintenance and Regeneration Center), Davis-Monthan AFB, Tucson, Arizona. Under the START (Strategic Arms Reduction Talks) treaties between the United States and the former USSR, 365 B-52s were designated for scrapping. The center uses a 13,000-pound (5,910-kilogram) guillotine to cut up the airframes once they are stripped of all useful parts.

can be serviced. The work orders for each B-52H fill twenty-one loose-leaf notebooks.

There is an old air force joke among pilots that goes, "When the weight of the paperwork equals the weight of the plane, you can go fly." In the case of the B-52H, which weighs nearly half a million pounds (227,000 kilograms) when fully loaded, this saying is not that much of an exaggeration. The air force has kept extensive records, not only of each B-52's maintenance and modification but also of the actual flights for each plane dating from the 1970s. During every flight, crew members must keep detailed and accurate notes of everything, such as takeoff weight, weapons carried and released, changes in altitude and speed, and every landing and refueling. Until recently, all these records were kept on paper, but now crews record the information on a computer when the flight is completed.

In addition to the records, engineers also work out of an air force "boneyard," known as AMARC. This is a kind of airplane graveyard at Davis-Monthan Air Force Base in Tucson, Arizona. Here, the engineers study hundreds of B-52s that are no longer in service in a kind of working laboratory where they conduct "autopsies" of the old planes. These technicians test theories on everything from how to reduce wear and tear of the plane's parts to new, better, and faster repair methods.

The first B-52 was born out of the ashes of World War II. Its ancestors were the B-29 and B-47. Although the two had performed admirably during the war, military officials realized that in the event of a war against the Soviet Union or China, the United States needed a bomber that could travel longer distances so that it would not have to be based overseas. The planes also needed to carry larger bomb loads, including the new atomic weapons that had been used against the Japanese in Hiroshima and Nagasaki in August 1945.

The air force turned to the Boeing Military Airplane Company with the project. Boeing, which had already built the highly successful B-17 and B-29, agreed to take on the task of designing the next generation of bombers.

An Uncertain Beginning

Almost from the beginning, however, the B-52 project was troubled. Early designs fell short of the ambitious vision that the air force had for the plane, and some military officials wondered if Boeing could succeed in designing a plane that would surpass the range, speed, altitude, and payload capabilities of the older bombers. Still, air force officials told Boeing to keep trying in the hope that a workable design would soon emerge. Despite this vote of confidence, Boeing came close to losing the project three times. It would take a last-ditch effort during a long weekend in October 1948, when a group of Boeing engineers working with Colonel Pete Warden, chief of bomb development for the air force, drafted a new design. What finally emerged from that meeting was one of the most enduring bombers ever conceived.

A B-52 being built at a Boeing airplane factory in Wichita, Kansas, on December 5, 1955. The plane you see above is the first ever built at Boeing's Kansas factory and was completed fourteen years after the bombing of Pearl Harbor. In the background, B-47s are being built. The B-47 would be decommissioned several years later, when it was replaced by the B-52.

Scrapping the idea of a plane with turboprops, the engineers decided to use jet engines and deeply angled wings, making a plane that could fly faster and smoother than existing models. The plane's bomb bay, or storage area, was designed to carry the limousine-sized atomic weapons that were also currently being developed. With its huge fuel tanks located in the wings and fuselage, the plane would be able to fly long distances, which, in the event of war, allowed it to strike deep within the Soviet Union or China. Designing the plane with the ability to refuel in the air guaranteed it an almost limitless range; theoretically, the B-52 could circle the globe in continuous flight.

On November 29, 1951, the first B-52 rolled out of the Boeing hangar in Seattle, Washington. Covered with giant tarpaulins, the plane got ready for its maiden flight. While still undergoing its preflight testing, the plane's primary power source suffered a massive failure and

NEW RECORDS

On January 10 and 11, 1962, a B-52H from the 4136th Strategic Wing in Minot AFB set a new straight line distance record by completing an 12,532.28-mile (approximately 20,177 kilometers) nonstop, unrefueled flight from Kadena, Okinawa, to Torrejon, Spain. This broke the previous record of 11,235 miles (18,080 kilometers) set in 1946 by the U.S. Navy Lockheed P2V Neptune Truculent Turtle. Thirty-three years later, on August 25, 1995, a B-52H established a new speed record for aircraft weighing between 440,000 and 550,000 pounds (199,584 and 249,480 kilograms) by flying 6,200 miles (10,000 kilometers) with a payload of 11,000 pounds (5,000 kilograms) in eleven hours and twenty-three minutes at an average speed of 556 miles per hour (895 kilometers per hour).

ripped out part of a wing. It seemed another sign that the project, estimated to have cost $8 million for the single prototype, a huge sum in 1951, was doomed. The plane was quickly returned to its construction area in an attempt to correct the problem. It would be close to six months before the B-52 would at last get off the ground.

Introducing the B-52

The success of subsequent test flights indicated that Boeing had done something right. From then on, there was no looking back. Boeing started production of the B-52 line, which continued throughout the next decade. Eventually, there would be eight different models: the B-52A, B, C, D, E, F, G, and H, the current B-52. Each new model offered improvements and modifications that made it capable of flying farther and handling heavier loads than its predecessor.

The first B-52H, which was made in Wichita, Kansas, flew on July 20, 1960. Delivery of the B-52H to operational units began on May 9, 1961, when the 379th Bombardment Wing at Wurtsmith Air Force Base (AFB) in Michigan received its first aircraft. The last B-52H was delivered to the 4136th Strategic Wing Command at Minot AFB in North Dakota on October 26, 1962, bringing production of the

Stratofortress to an end. Boeing built a total of 102 planes in this series.

The most noticeable difference between the B-52H and earlier versions was the replacement of the water-injected turbo jet engines with turbofans by Pratt & Whitney. The new engines offered 30 percent more thrust, providing for better airfield performance and an extra margin of safety during heavyweight takeoffs. In addition, the engines were much cleaner and quieter when operating at full power, and thus more environmentally friendly than the older engines, which left behind trails of noxious black smoke. Because the engine is quieter, the cabin decks are less noisy and crews are less likely to become tired.

At the time when the Stratofortress made its maiden flight in 1952, no one knew that these planes would prove so invaluable to U.S. military efforts for decades to come.

Hot Planes for a Cold War

For the first ten years of its service, the B-52 bomber, including the current B-52H series, officially known as the Stratofortress, operated in the tense environment of the Cold War. At the peak of the Cold War, to avoid being caught on the ground in the event of a nuclear attack, the planes were kept airborne, carrying their payload of bombs twenty-four hours a day for almost a decade. Crews lived for days in bomb-proof underground bunkers and slept in their flight suits so as to be ready if they were called to duty. If called, they only needed to slip on their special steel and glass helmets while racing down the runway to their planes. While those flights had ended by the early 1960s, the B-52s were kept on ready alert until 1991. With five airborne command posts, prepared to direct a war from the air, B-52s were kept in the sky in constant rotation.

By 1963, the Air Force Strategic Air Command (SAC), located near Omaha, Nebraska, oversaw the operations of 650 B-52s deployed among forty-two squadrons at thirty-eight air bases throughout the United States. Aided by additional air refueling bases in the South Pacific, such as Andersen AFB in Guam, the B-52s could strike virtually any target in the Soviet Union or China. This deployment would remain in place until

The ground offensive of the Vietnam conflict took place underneath a heavy canopy of jungle foliage, making it difficult to see Vietcong troops from above. A common remedy for this was carpet bombing, the deployment of a large number of bombs over an area where enemy troops were suspected to be hiding. B-52s dropped over 2.5 million tons (2,267,960 metric tons) of bombs over Vietnam, Cambodia, and Laos during the conflict.

The Strategic Air Command (SAC) in Omaha, Nebraska. Shown here in 1965, SAC was built during the Cold War. The United States had a nuclear arsenal unmatched by any other country in the world, most of it under the control of SAC, which was constantly on the alert for a possible nuclear strike. B-52s and their pilots waited around the clock for the SAC command to launch a counterstrike. Closed down after the fall of the Soviet Union, the sign outside SAC read "Peace is our Profession."

the early 1990s, when the collapse of the Soviet Union made it no longer necessary to maintain such a high state of alert.

Besides remaining on alert for a potential conflict with the Soviet Union, the B-52D, F, and G series were used in more conventional ways during the Vietnam War. On June 18, 1965, for instance, B-52s struck targets in Vietnam for the first time, providing much needed support for American ground forces. The SAC B-52s based in Guam and Thailand began conducting Operation Arc Light, which consisted of carpet-bombing raids on Vietcong strongholds in South Vietnam, Laos, and Cambodia. In 1972, SAC B-52s began an eleven-day series of strategic bombing missions (known as Operation Linebacker) against Hanoi, the capital of North Vietnam—an action that paved the way for a peace agreement in 1973.

With eight engines and a wingspan of 185 feet (56.3 meters), this B-52 Stratofortress soars majestically through the air. An awe-inspiring sight, the B-52 has defied all expectations and acquired a proven track record unmatched by any bomber before or since. There are three ALCMs under each wing, meaning that together with the eight ALCMs in the weapons bay, a total of fourteen ALCMs were carried on this mission.

This B-52G takes off on a mission that will bring it to the heart of the conflict in Operation Desert Storm, where it will log a lot of flight hours as the main bomber used by the UN coalition forces. Nine 500-pound (227-kilogram) Mark 82 bombs are attached under each wing.

The B-52G was the first U.S. aircraft launched in the 1991 Gulf War against Iraq, where its reliability rate was even higher than during operations in Vietnam. B-52s struck wide-area troop concentrations, fixed installations, and bunkers, destroying the morale of Iraq's Republican Guard. The Gulf War involved what was then the longest strike mission in the history of aerial warfare, when B-52s took off from Barksdale Air Force Base in Louisiana, flew to Iraq, launched conventional air-launched cruise missiles, and returned to Barksdale—a nonstop thirty-five-hour combat mission.

Enter the B-52H

The B-52H made its combat debut on September 3, 1996, when a pair of B-52Hs launched thirteen AGM-86C cruise missiles against targets in southern Iraq. This attack was in response to Iraqi president Saddam Hussein's military assault against the northern town of Arbil on August 30. The B-52H attack originated from Guam, with the aircraft refueling in midair four times.

In all, the B-52s flew 1,620 missions in the Gulf War. The ultimate compliment to the effectiveness of the plane came from an Iraqi general who defected to Saudi Arabia early in the conflict. He explained that he defected because he had seen the effect of the B-52s. When U.S. military intelligence officers checked the records, they determined that the general's division had never been hit by a B-52. His reply: his brother's division had been. It was one of many examples of how B-52s completely demoralized the Iraqi army.

Today, the B-52H fleet has been consolidated at two bases: Barksdale Air Force Base in Louisiana and Minot Air Force Base in North Dakota. Flight training, however, takes place in Alaska and at the Tonopah Test Range in Nevada. Periodic training and recertification inspections are conducted at the home bases. There are a total of ninety-two B-52H aircraft remaining in service, with seventy-one of those planes assigned to nuclear weapons missions. However, budgetary cuts in 1996 have led to a need for further reductions, which will eventually bring the B-52H fleet down to sixty-six. Twelve aircraft at Minot Air Force Base were deactivated late in 1996. Four more at Barksdale Air Force Base will also be retired. All retired aircraft are sent to AMARC, the B-52 "boneyard" in Tucson, Arizona.

THE WARRIOR THAT FIGHTS FOR A HUNDRED YEARS

The air force, continuing to work with Boeing, constantly experiments with ways to improve and revitalize the B-52H, which has proven itself well worth the investment in time and money.

Those who fly in the B-52H planes have high hopes for the plane's future. As one flyer who spent eight years flying BUFFs for SAC and who is now employed as a test pilot put it in the *Popular Mechanic* article "New Life for BUFF" by William Garvey: "Someday, if they haven't already, people will get together to share some of their memories of the B-52. I believe there will be a family with four generations who have worked on the airplane. And the only constraint on more generations will be our mortality."

Lt. General Thomas J. Keck *(center)* gives the thumbs-up during the B-52's 50th anniversary celebration at the New York Stock Exchange on April 15, 2002.

Brigadier General Guy Townsend, one of the pilots on the B-52's first flight in 1952, agrees. The B-52H, he says, could go on indefinitely. As Townsend says in "New Life for BUFF": "It boggles the mind. Right now, there are three generations of pilots who have flown that plane—

NOT JUST A PLANE ANYMORE

The B-52 has not only shaped modern military history, it has also found its way into American popular culture. During the 1960s, a hairstyle fashionable among young women, the beehive, was nicknamed the "B-52." The hairstyle consisted of a large bouffant that required considerable amounts of hair-spray to keep in place. The nickname arose because the hair's conical shape had an appearance similar to the nose of a B-52. In the late 1970s, a popular rock band borrowed the name. The two female members of the B-52s wore their hair in that style.

grandfather, father, and son—in the same family. If it lasts until 2040 [as air force projections suggest it will], five generations will have flown the same plane." That's quite a legacy for a plane that almost never made it off the ground.

The BUFF Family

The pilots and crew of the B-52H work together as a tightly knit unit. It is not uncommon for the crew members to socialize with each other even when they are not on duty. Crew members who become ill will still report to work in order not to miss a mission. Their loyalty to the plane and to each other is so strong that both pilots and crewmen have turned down higher-paying jobs in order to stay with the B-52.

This sense of camaraderie has also allowed the pilots and crew of the B-52 to bend the rules a little. Sometimes after finishing a mission, pilots will set up special radio frequencies not monitored by the airbase, which allow them to talk freely with each other. One group was even known to play bingo on their way back from missions.

Because of its long service in the name of democracy, the B-52 has become a beloved symbol of U.S. military superiority. In downtown Shreveport, Louisiana, citizens gather around a 56-foot-long (17-meter) B-52 made of rectangular sheets of cake. Spectators were given icing to write messages on the cakes, which were provided to celebrate the fifty-second birthday of neighboring Barksdale Air Force Base.

Freedom by BUFF

In 1992, to commemorate the B-52's forty years of service, the air force issued a special cloth patch. The emblem, showing the classic silhouette of the B-52 against a background of stars and stripes, reads, "40 Years–Freedom by BUFF." At the time, the air force had slated the B-52 for retirement and wanted to remember the plane and the people associated with it in a special way.

Ten years later, the B-52H is still going strong. Cuts in the defense budget that forced a reduction in the number of B-52s also ensured that the plane survived the budget cuts. Financially, designing and building a fleet of bombers to replace the B-52 would be too expensive. It was more economical to refit the older, durable B-52s and keep them in operation. On April 13, 2002, the air force

Although the air force estimates that the B-52 will be retired by 2040, all signs point to it going straight on ahead for even longer. With the ability to clock long flight hours and absorb new technology as it's being developed, chances are that we won't see the end of the B-52 for decades to come.

celebrated the official fiftieth anniversary of the B-52. The event was planned for six months and commemorated an airplane that one reporter in *Popular Mechanics* called "the warrior that will fight for 100 years." These days, especially in the aftermath of far more expensive and far less successful projects, no one in the U.S. government or military speaks of retiring the B-52H. If anything, they are already making plans about how to observe its seventy-fifth anniversary. As long as the United States needs them, the BUFFS will keep on flying.

GLOSSARY

Al Qaeda An international terrorist group founded in 1989 by Osama bin Laden. The group is dedicated to opposing non-Islamic governments with violence.

antiship Strikes against ships that can be launched from another ship or on land using planes or missiles.

battle assessment Information and statistics gathered on damage and casualties in a target area during a battle.

Cold War A period of intense rivalry between the United States and the Soviet Union that never developed into a war. The Cold War lasted from the end of World War II in 1945 until 1991, when the Soviet Union collapsed.

electronic warfare officer A person in charge of all devices used to confuse or suppress enemy radar and missiles.

haphazardly Randomly or without precision.

harboring Protecting or giving shelter to someone.

I-beam rack adapter A special beam or plate that is attached to an existing plane structure to carry heavier and longer bombs and missiles.

infrared A type of light that is invisible to the naked eye. In night flying, the infrared light is used in special scanning equipment to pick up infrared heat energy from surrounding objects.

land mine A large bomb or explosive device buried underground that explodes when a vehicle drives over it.

long-range Capable of traveling great distances.

payload The load carried by a vehicle that will be used for a specific purpose, such as bombs or missiles.

precision guided Missiles or bombs that are positioned by radar or laser designators for a direct hit on a target.

propaganda Written and/or illustrated material that is often highly distorted or unfair and that is used to persuade people toward a particular point of view.

pylon A rigid structure on the outside of an aircraft that can be used to support an engine or a missile.

retaliation To get back at or seek revenge against someone.

service ceiling A measurement usually applied to military planes based on the height above sea level at which an aircraft is unable to climb faster than a designated rate (in the United States, that rate is 100 feet per minute) under good weather conditions.

strategic Designed or planned to strike and destroy an enemy's ability to fight a war.

stronghold A fortress or place of refuge.

Taliban A movement formed in 1994 against the former governing power of Afghanistan. Taliban members believe in a fundamentalist form of the Islamic religion.

tarpaulin A piece of waterproof material such as canvas used to protect something from moisture.

tonnage Weight measured in tons.

wingspan The distance from the tip of one of a pair of wings to that of the other on an airplane.

FOR MORE INFORMATION

Air Combat Command
Office of Public Affairs
115 Thompson Street, Suite 211
Langley AFB, VA 23665-1987
(757) 764-5007

Federation of American Scientists
1717 K Street NW, Suite 209
Washington, DC 20036
(202) 546-3300
Web site: http://www.fas.org/index.html

Office of the Assistant Secretary of Defense for Public Affairs
    OASD(PA)PIA
1400 Defense Pentagon, Room 3A750
Washington, DC 20301-1400
(703) 697-5737
Web site: http://www.defenselink.mil

U.S. Air Force
Public Affairs Resource Library
1690 Air Force Pentagon
Washington, DC 20330-1690
Web site: http://www.af.mil/lib/faqs.shtml

Web Sites

Due to the changing nature of Internet links, the Rosen Publishing Group, Inc., has developed an online list of Web sites related to the subject of this book. This site is updated regularly. Please use this link to access the list:

http://www.rosenlinks.com/usw/b5st/

FOR FURTHER READING

Chant, Christopher. *Military Aircraft*. Philadelphia: Chelsea House
 Publishers, 1999.

Chant, Christopher. *The Role of the Fighter & Bomber.* Philadelphia:
 Chelsea House Publishers, 1999.

Holden, Henry. *Air Force Aircraft*. Springfield, NJ: Enslow
 Publishers, 2001.

BIBLIOGRAPHY

Birnbaum, Jeffrey. "Happy Birthday, B-52." *Fortune*, January 2002. Retrieved March 2002 (http://www.business2.com/articles/mag/0,1640,36877,FF.html).

Boyne, Walter. *Boeing B-52: A Documentary History.* London, England: Jane's Publishing Company, 1981.

Davis, Larry. *B-52 Stratofortress in Action (Aircraft, No 130).* Lemming: MN: Squadron/Signal Publishers, 1993.

Dorr, Robert F., and Lindsay Peacock. *B-52 Stratofortress: Boeing's Cold Warrior.* New York: Motorbooks, 1995.

Erwin, Sandra L. "B-52 Bombers Upgraded with Advanced Radios." *National Defense*, March 13, 2002. Retrieved March 2002 (http://www.nationaldefensemagazine.org/article.cfm?Id=756).

Fishman, Charles. "Fresh Start 2002: Nonstop Flight." *Fast Company* magazine. Retrieved March 2002 (http://www.fastcompany.com/online/54/B52.html).

Francillon, Rene J., and Peter B. Lewis. *B-52: Aging BUFFs, Youthful Crews.* London, England: Osprey Publishing Limited, 1988.

Garvey, William. "New Life for BUFF." *Popular Mechanics*, March 1999. Retrieved March 2002 (http://popularmechanics.com/popmech/sci9903STMIBM.html).

Hirsh, Michael, and Roy Gutman. "Warlords and B-52s." *Newsweek*, March 4, 2002, pp.28–29.

Koch, Andrew. "Air and Missile Strikes Herald New Phase in the Fight Against Terrorism." *Jane's Defence Weekly*, October 7, 2001. Retrieved March 2002 (http://www.janes.com/security/international_security/news/jdw/jdw011007_1_n.shtml).

Lefforge, Lt. Col. Douglas. "Keck: Bombers 'Writing Airpower History.'" Air Combat Command News Service. December 31, 2001. Retrieved March 2002 (http://www2.acc.af.mil/accnews/dec01/01454.html).

Lefforge, Lt. Col. Douglas. "Wing Flies 400th Combat Sortie." Air Combat Command News Service. January 23, 2002. Retrieved March 2002 (http://www2.acc.af.mil/accnews/jan02/02024.html).

Sweetman, Bill. "The B-52." *Popular Science*, March 10, 2002. Retrieved March 2002 (http://www.popsci.com/popsci/aviation/article/0,12543,194509-1,00.html).

Wilson, Stewart. *Boeing B-47, B-52 and Avro Vulcan.* New York: Motorbooks, 1997.

INDEX

CREDITS

About the Author

Meg Greene is a writer and historian who grew up not far from SAC headquarters in Omaha, Nebraska. She received a B.S. in history from Lindenwood College, an M.A. in history from the University of Nebraska at Omaha, and an M.S. in historic preservation from the University of Vermont. She is the author of fourteen books and serves as contributing editor of "History for Children" at Suite101.com. Ms. Greene makes her home in Virginia.

Photo Credits

Cover, pp. 4, 8, 17, 21, 38 © David Halford; p. 6 © Philip Wallick; pp. 9, 19, 27, 35, 37 © AP/Wide World Photos; p. 11 © Master Sergeant Ralph Hallmon/US Air Force; p. 13 © AFP Photo/Corbis; pp. 16, 18 © George Hall/Corbis; p. 22 © Joseph Sohm/Corbis; pp. 25, 29 Bettmann/Corbis; p. 28 © Hulton/Archive/Getty Images, Inc.; pp. 30–31 © US Air Force; p. 32 © Corbis; p. 34 © Stocktreck/Corbis; p. 36 © Lynn Goldsmith/Corbis.

Layout and Design

Thomas Forget

Editor

Annie Sommers